Truro
Cornwall

Hi there,

My name is Toby, and I am a Dalmatian.

My walker (human) takes me on loads of lovely walks that
are just perfect for dogs. My doggy friends and I were
wondering if all our canine buddies knew about these
walks. So, I decided to sit down and write a guide.
As I love to play, I will try and let you know if you are likely
to meet any other dogs to play with or to sniff.
I will try and let you know about all the good things and
any not so good features of any walk.
I will also let you know if there are any poo bins for your
walker, as they don't seem to like poo as much as we do.
If you know of any walks that I don't know about, let me
know so I can check them out and possibly include them
in the next book. If you send me a picture of yourself I'll
put it with your walk.

Enjoy your new walks,

Toby
Email me: toby@scrivenhousebooks.co.uk

Walk 1 - Polruan-Boddinick-Fowey

Grid Reference: 125 507   Landranger 204/201   Distance: 5 miles (3 hours)

This is a truly fabulous walk, one of my favourites so far. There are a few steep bits on the footpath that can be slippery when very wet. I would recommend wellies on this one.

1. Drive to Polruan and park in the car park signposted on the left at the top of the steep hill down to the harbour. The sign says that the car park overlooks the harbour. Now walk down to Polruan Harbour. If you don't have any cash on you, my walkers go to the pub and use the cash machine before setting off.
2. Follow signs that point towards the Hall Walk that leads out of Polruan up the river. The path eventually takes you into the woods. Now simply follow the path through the woods enjoying all the views along the way. Ignore the path signposted on the left with a squirrel engraved post.
3. You will come to a small road. Turn right up the road, and then after about 5 metres turn left to rejoin the path through the next woods. You will find a cute little waterfall in these woods if it has been raining.
4. Eventually the footpath leads into a field which seems to be a new addition to the route. The path down the field can get quite slippery, so you can walk down the road if you prefer, but do get your walkers to put you on your lead.
5. At the bottom of the hill there is a deep track that leads left towards the river. This takes you to a lovely little hamlet with a wooden bridge over the river. Cross the bridge and follow the footpath signs on the opposite side.
6. As you climb up the opposite hill from the river the path takes a sharp turn to the left. Please get your walker to put you on your lead as this is farmland for a few hundred metres. You climb up the steep hill out of the woods and then walk along the bottom of a field for a minute of so before returning back into the woods on the left.
7. Now you just continue following the path through the woods. After a while you will reach a magnificent monument, magnificent because of the amazing view of Polruan and Fowey. There is also a shelter here for a rainy day picnic. Once you have soaked up the view continue on to Bodinnick.

8. In Bodinnick, head downhill to the ferry slipway and await the ferry. It is normally 90p for each foot passenger (Feb 2007). The ferry can be a bit noisy when it starts and stops pulling the chains. I didn't like it much but it is a very quick journey and worth it for a bit of my walker's pasty in Fowey.
9. Once off the ferry, head left into Fowey, enjoy some window shopping and some pasties. You could have a spot of lunch in one of the pub beer gardens on a nice day.
10. When you have had a good sniff around Fowey, make your way to the Town Quay. Here you can catch the Foot Passenger Ferry to Polruan. They are happy to take dogs and charge 20p to make us feel part of the whole experience. I would definitely get your walker to put you on the lead, just in case the temptation to chase seagulls ends in a big splash.
11. Once back in Polruan it is a slow amble up the steep hill back to the car park. If you turn left up School Lane you will get there a bit more quickly.

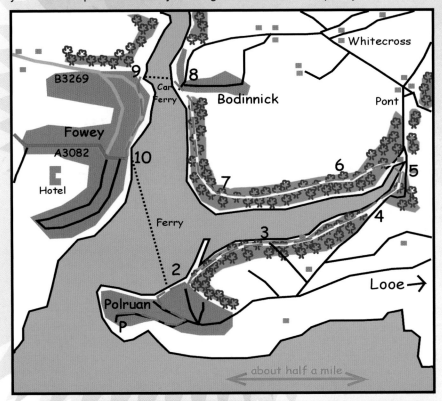

Playmates?	Y	Water to play in?	Y	Running space?	Y
Are there any hills?	Y	Any tricky stiles?	N	Car Parking?	Y
Are farm animals likely?	N	Poo Bins?	Y	Plenty of sticks?	Y

Walk 2 - Tintagel Waterfall

| Grid Reference: 045 703 | Landranger 200 | Distance: 2 miles (1.5 hours) |

This is a lovely river walk with an amazing waterfall and tea room at the far end and great sea views at the start. Be warned that the tea room and access to the waterfall is only open 7 days a week Easter to October. However the walk is lovely any time of year. St Nectan's waterfall has been described as amongst the ten most important spiritual sites in the country. The Kieve has been a place of reverence, worship and healing since pre-Christian times. People of many faiths have walked the ancient route to the waterfall to bathe in its mysterious and therapeutic atmosphere.

1. From Tintagel take the coast road B3263 towards Boscastle. A couple of minutes outside Tintagel the road drops steeply and then climbs quickly out of the Rocky Valley. As the road levels you will see a small car park on the left which is for walkers up to the waterfall. Park here. Make sure your walkers put you on the lead, as the road can get busy in the summer.
2. Now walk up the road another 10 metres and then cross over and follow the footpath signs for St Nectan's Waterfall.
3. After 20 metres a lane leads off to the right. Follow this enjoying the views out over the sea and the farmland. My walkers normally let me off my lead now.
4. Eventually the lane starts to drop down the hill, near the bottom, a track leads down to the river on your right. Follow this track all the way up the valley.
5. After a while you will climb quite a few steps (my walkers lost count). These take you up to the tea rooms. If you are in the holiday season you can stop for a cuppa and a cream tea and then head down some more steps to see the waterfall.
6. Out of season you can call the Tea Room owners and make an appointment to visit the waterfall to save disappointment. The number is 01840 770760 or Email: barry@stnectan.fsnet.co.uk. Be warned there is an admission charge to the waterfall of £3 per adult (at time of printing)
7. Once you have finished you can return the way you came.

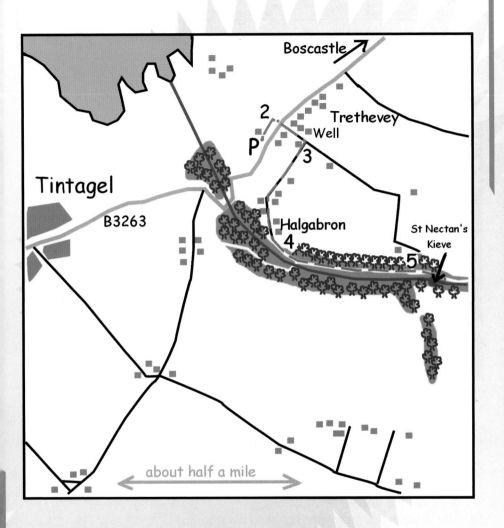

Playmates?	Y	Water to play in?	Y	Running space?	N
Are there any hills?	Y	Any tricky stiles?	N	Car Parking?	Y
Are farm animals likely?	N	Poo Bins?	N	Plenty of sticks?	Y

Walk 3 - King's Wood

| Grid reference: 007 488 | Landranger 204 | Distance: 2 miles (1.5 hours) |

This is a woodland walk with loads of history, apparently the wood used to belong to Thomas Earl of Lancaster who was one of the most powerful men in England at the time. He was cousin to Edward II and led the Baron's Revolt in 1332. Unfortunately they lost and he was beheaded. He probably rode the same tracks you are walking on, over 600 years ago!

1. From St Austell, take the B3273 towards Mevagissey. After about 3 miles you wi see the King's Wood car park on your left, over a little bridge. Pull in and park up I would get your walkers to put you on a lead as the Mevagissey road is still quit nearby.
2. With your back to the road, turn left out of the car park following the stream back up towards St. Austell. Stick to the path by the stream rather than the one that goes into the woods.
3. After a while this path turns right into the woods and then forks. Take the right fork signposted to King's Wood. You come to a rough car park. Take the track that leads up to the left, not the one straight on (you will rejoin this later).
4. Follow the track as it winds up the hill into the woods, this is a long steady climb. Eventually the track will bare right and open out into a large clearing with a couple of benches and some nice views.
5. Take the small track that leads up left out of the clearing.
6. Then take the next track that goes off right and then takes you down quite a steep slope with a few rough steps. You will then join a more substantial track that leads up from the car park you came to earlier.

6. Turn left and then almost immediately right up some wood and earth steps, and then follow the field boundary along the top of the woods. You will follow this for a long while.
7. Eventually you will pass the wrecked gamekeeper's cottage and the path will turn right and descend downhill. Keep following the path downhill rather than any right turns back into the woods.
8. The path should take you around the left hand side of a very muddy little lake and over a little bridge. Once over the bridge the path bares right and then left and ambles its way through a lovely bit of woodland. You should cross two small footbridges.
9. Beware. The last footbridge brings you out onto a cycle path that can be busy in the summer so get your walkers to put you on the lead for a couple of minutes so you don't run under a bike.
10. Turn right and follow the cycle path back up to the car park.

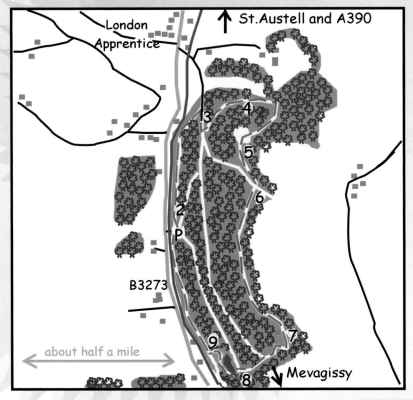

Playmates?	Y	Water to play in?	Y	Running space?	Y
Are there any hills?	Y	Any tricky stiles?	N	Car Parking?	Y
Are farm animals likely?	N	Poo Bins?	Y	Plenty of sticks?	Y

Walk 4 - Idless Wood

Grid reference: 820 478   Landranger 204   Distance: 3 miles (2 hrs)

You can either have a gentle stroll by the river and turn back, or, you can do a longer circular walk with a steady uphill climb. From our experience it is worth keeping one eye open for mountain bikes at the weekend. However, there is plenty of room for everyone!

1. From Truro head through the town and follow signs for Boscastle and the B3284. You will come to a roundabout on the outskirts of the town with no real signs. If you do, bare right up the hill up Kenwyn Road. Before you get out of Truro you need to keep a sharp eye out for a small sign pointing right for Idless this should send you up Higher Trehaverne Road. Now follow the lane through Idless and take the right turn when the road forks, following the River Allen up the valley. Keep an eye out on your right for a turn into Idless Woods car park. Find a place to park and then head up the main track that leads up the hill from the main car parking area (the woods are called St Clements Woods on the OS maps).

2. Follow the main track up the hill. At the obvious fork you have a decision to make. You can either go right, and walk along the River Allen and turn back to the car park when you have had enough or you can go left up the hill. We went left.

3. Follow the track on through the woods, it goes on a long way. Eventually the track clearly narrows and goes downhill. At the bottom of the hill there is a crossroads in the track.

4. Turn right and take the steep track down to the River Allen. At the bottom of the hill the track forks.

5. Take the right fork and then follow this track all the way back to the car park. It will turn away from the river and up hill a little bit at the end, just keep following.

Playmates?	Y	Water to play in?	Y	Running space?	Y
Are there any hills?	Y	Any tricky stiles?	N	Car Parking?	Y
Are farm animals likely?	N	Poo Bins?	Y	Plenty of sticks?	Y

Walk 5 - Up the Looe

Grid reference: 252 538   Landranger 201   Distance: 2 miles (1.5 hours)

This is a lovely walk up the West Looe Valley. We did it early on a sunny morning and the scenery and wildlife were breathtaking. There are a few steep flights of steps on this walk. I take my walkers on the longest (red) route which was hard work. However, there are a few options to shorten the walk.

1. Drive to Looe and park in the huge public car park on the west side of the river. If your walker parks at the far end of the car park it means less time on the lead around noisy cars. The car park will cost you around £2 depending on how long you are gone, but well worth it!
2. Park up and head off into Watergate Woods. There is a sign available with a map so you decide which of the three main walks you would like to do. Try not to get paw marks on the map as you are reading it.
3. We followed the red route through the woods. The markers were brilliant, so you just need to follow these. It was tempting to follow a sign that said low tide route to Watergate, but we thought better of it as the tide was coming in.
4. This is a lovely walk to stop and have a picnic on. Watergate is lovely and a great place to have a break. We saw egrets, swans, ducks and herons during our short rest stop.
5. On the way back there are a few climbs, but none as hard as the climb out of Watergate. If your walkers think it is too much you can follow the road out of Watergate and then take a left back into the woods along the Bridle Path. Less of a scramble up the woods.
6. Follow the red markers back home, and take the Bridle Path that runs on your left parallel to the path, if you have had enough of steps!
7. The paths all end up on a road that can be quite busy in high summer, so get back on the lead and head left back towards the car park.

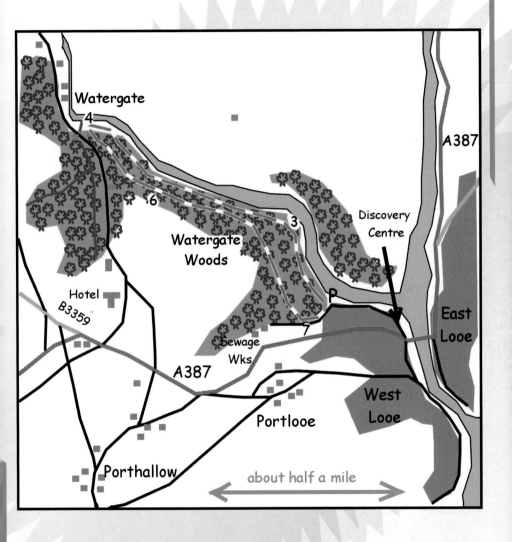

Playmates?	Y	Water to play in?	Y	Running space?	Y
Are there any hills?	Y	Any tricky stiles?	N	Car Parking?	Y
Are farm animals likely?	N	Poo Bins?	Y	Plenty of sticks?	Y

Walk 6 - The Luxulyan Valley

Grid reference: 073 562   Landranger 200   Distance: 3 miles (2.5 hours)

This is a fantastic walk with a few surprises on the way. It wasn't marked on the map as anything special, now it's one of my favourite walks.

1. Take the A390 from St Blazey to Lostwithiel, as you come up a steep hill out of St. Blazey the road turns into two lanes on your side. Keep your eyes peeled and you will see a small turning on the left signposted to Ponts Mill. Take this turn and drive to the end and park in the car park on the left.
2. Now head up the wide track that runs up river. It has a Luxulyan Valley marker post at the start. There is a great little weather station on the telegraph pole here which is worth a quick look. It made my walkers laugh.
3. As you round the corner the path divides in two, one half goes under the railway the other half goes uphill. Take the right hand uphill route. This is an old inclined tramway built by a man called Treffy in the 1800's.
4. Follow the track all the way up, passing under a lovely arched footbridge on the way.
5. You eventually come to a point where a very obvious leat runs across the path. Turn left here and follow the leat along through the woods.
6. At one point you will notice a huge structure up on your right in the woods. It used to house a massive waterwheel that powered trams up and down the incline you just walked up (I bet you wish they were still running, I did!)
7. After you have had a sniff around, rejoin the leat path and follow it along through the woods. Down below you will probably hear the River Par crashing down the valley.

8. Finally you will reach a huge via/aquaduct built again by Treffy. You can go up and walk across the top (Just walk on down the path you are on until you see a bridge on your right. Cross the bridge and follow the path up to the top. The Viaduct carried trams across the valley, and also carried water in an aquaduct hidden inside).

9. Come back the way you came and rejoin the track you were on, and continue the short distance to the car park. There is a sign here that tells you all the information that I have told you, but in more detail for your walkers.

10. Once they have read themselves silly you can encourage them to turn around and head back on the lower path that follows the road back under the aqua/viaduct. All you need to do now is just stick to this path and it will take you all the way back down the valley to the car park at the start.

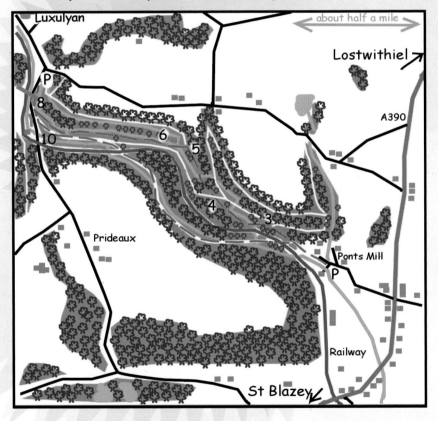

Playmates?	Y	Water to play in?	Y	Running space?	Y
Are there any hills?	Y	Any tricky stiles?	N	Car Parking?	Y
Are farm animals likely?	N	Poo Bins?	Y	Plenty of sticks?	Y

Walk 7 - Tremayne Woods

Grid Reference: 731 249   Landranger 204   Distance: 2 miles (1.5 hours)

A fantastic little walk tucked away on the banks of the beautiful River Helford. There are a couple of lovely spots along the way for sun drenched picnics and even a swim in the river (if you are brave, I prefer to just paddle!)

1. From Falmouth follow the back lanes to Constantine and then onto Gweek. Once you are through Gweek follow signs to St.Keverne on the B3293. From Helston take the A3083 towards The Lizard and then turn off onto the B3293 towards St.Keverne. Once on the B3293 look for a left turn towards Newtown-St-Martin, continue through the village and on through the next village, St Martin. As you go down the hill keep an eye out for a small lane to your right, opposite signs to a campsite. Follow this lane down a steep winding hill. At a sharp left hand corner you will see the entrance to Tremayne Woods on your left. Park up without obstructing the farmer's entrance opposite.
2. Now all you have to do is wander down the path into Tremayne Woods. As you get to the bottom of the hill the bridle path carries on around the valley side. Take the footpath on your left that follows the little stream down to the river. This path leads you down through the woods and curls round to cross the stream over a little clapper bridge and then brings you up to rejoin the bridle path.
3. Turn left when you rejoin the bridle path and carry on into the first clearing.
4. I would take a left here and cross the clearing to the river bank. You get amazing views down the Helford River from here. You can then climb back up to the path and carry on through the woods.
5. Eventually you will descend to a small quay where you can have a picnic and enjoy a swim.
6. When you have finished follow the path back up to the car.

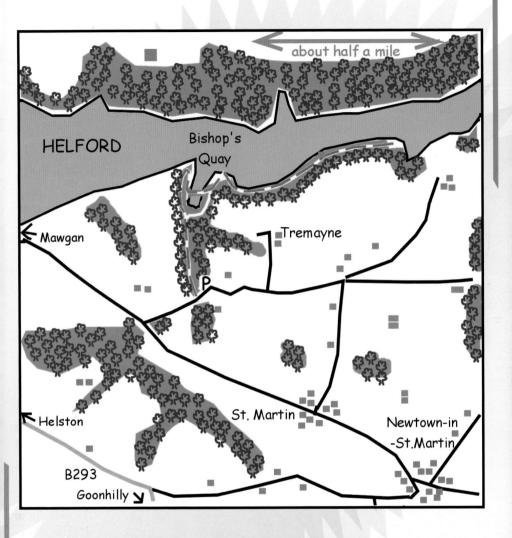

Playmates?	Y	Water to play in?	Y	Running space?	Y
Are there any hills?	Y	Any tricky stiles?	N	Car Parking?	N
Are farm animals likely?	N	Poo Bins?	N	Plenty of sticks?	Y

Walk 8 - Godolphin Woods

| Grid Reference: 599 325 | Landranger 203 | Distance: 1 mile (45mins) |

This is a really varied walk with water, woods and lovely woodland houses. A little gem tucked away in the West of Cornwall!

1. If you take the B3280 from Redruth towards Penzance, you will pass through Leedstown, and then get to Townshend. At Townshend turn right signposted to Godolphin House. After about 5 minutes you will go over a bridge over a small river the road will then turn left up a hill. As the road climbs you will see a wood in front of you with a stile in a stone wall and a metal gate. This is the entrance to part of the National Trust woods. Turn left down a gravel road following some very small National Trust car park signs. You will reach a stream at the bottom with a wooden footbridge crossing it, follow the road right, then follow the sign right into a small car park. Park up and head back to the wooden footbridge.
2. Cross the wooden bridge and turn left down the footpath along the River Hayle until you reach the other wooden bridge at the other end (if you come out on the road you have missed the bridge it is about 20 metres up the river). Cross the second wooden bridge and turn left back up the river towards the carpark.
3. When you reach the car park turn right up the gravel road towards the main road. You may need to get your walker to put your lead on near the top.
4. At the top turn left into the woods. There is a National Trust sign welcoming you here. Follow the track through the woods. You will pass the Godolphin Counting House. Keep following the track straight on through the woods.
5. You will cross a lovely wooden bridge where there is lovely water to play in.
6. Eventually the track bears right and comes to a T-junction with a large track/rough road. Take a right at the junction and follow the large track.
7. Further along the track you will see two waymarker arrows directing you right into the woods, follow the arrows right. This is a beautiful spot for a quick drink and stick chew. Follow the path as it winds through the woods, ignoring smaller tracks that branch off. Eventually you will reach the small wooden bridge again. Turn left and walk back along the path past the Counting House, and out to the main road. Then turn right down towards the car park.

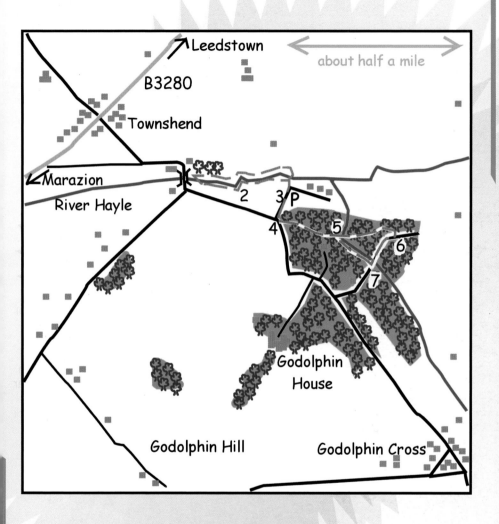

Playmates?	Y	Water to play in?	Y	Running space?	Y
Are there any hills?	Y	Any tricky stiles?	N	Car Parking?	Y
Are farm animals likely?	N	Poo Bins?	N	Plenty of sticks?	Y

Walk 9a - Padstow Beach

Grid Reference: 915 770   Landranger 200   Distance: 2 miles (1 hour)

I have included my two favourite beaches where dogs are welcome all year round, and can enjoy paddles in the water, a run on the sand and where the scenery is beautiful.

PADSTOW -Head out of the town following the River Camel towards the sea. You will then join the coast path. After a while there is a sloping path down to the beach. Ignore this as this leads to St.Georges Well , and there is a dog ban for this part of the beach from Easter to October the 1st. Carry on along the footpath which takes you around to some sand dunes. Then take the path into the dunes and onto the large beach. This is Harbour Cove, there is no beach ban here.

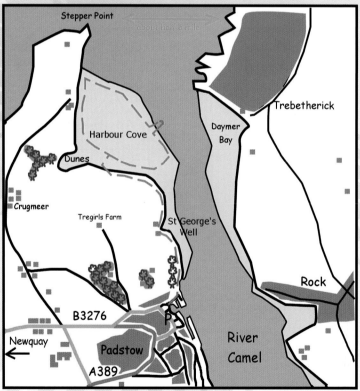

Playmates?	Y	Water to play in?	Y	Running space?	Y
Are there any hills?	Y	Any tricky stiles?	N	Car Parking?	Y
Are farm animals likely?	N	Poo Bins?	Y	Plenty of sticks?	N

Walk 9b - Gwenver Beach

Grid Reference: 363 277   Landranger 203   Distance: 0.5 miles (30 mins)

GWENVER - Gwenver is a gorgeous little beach tucked away around the corner from Sennen Cove. From the A30 look out for signs on the right for Tregiffian Farm. Follow this lane along avoiding left turns. You will eventually reach a privately owned cliff top car park on your left. Pull in, pay and park. Then enjoy the stunning views before descending the steps to Gwenver. I loved jumping in the surf here.

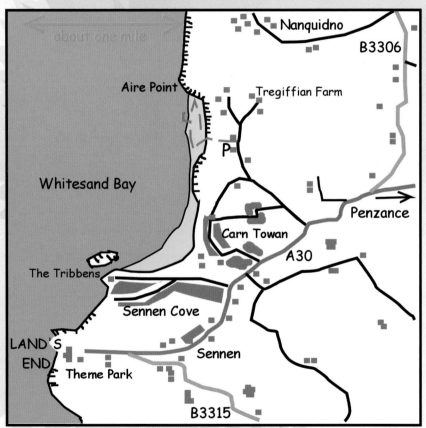

Playmates?	Y	Water to play in?	Y	Running space?	Y
Are there any hills?	YY	Any tricky stiles?	N	Car Parking?	Y
Are farm animals likely?	N	Poo Bins?	Y	Plenty of sticks?	N

Walk 10 - Coast Path to Porthcurnow

| Grid Reference: 418 239 | Landranger 203 | Distance: 6 miles (3.5 hrs) |

In an area with very few woodland walks we felt we needed to find a decent long walk for doggies like me who like lots of exercise, so we headed for the coast path. My walkers liked this route because it ends in Porthcurnow where there are pasties, pubs and the Minack Theatre. You can also opt to get a bus back if you don't want to do the return journey. However, they are infrequent and you should check timetables before deciding on this course of action.

1. From Penzance take the A30 towards Land's End. Then take the B3283 to St. Buryan. Go straight through St.Buryan following signs for Porthcurnow. At Sparnon take a sharp right onto the B3315 towards Lamorna and Mousehole. The road drops into one valley and then climbs up past Treverven House. You will reach the brow of the hill and start dropping into the next valley. You will see Trevedran Farm on your right.
2. Find somewhere to park on the left and then follow the footpath that starts by the roadside at the bottom of this small valley. The footpath follows the stream down to St.Loy's Cove (my walkers love the cream teas available here!)
3. Once you get near the cove the path forks down to the cove (and cream teas) or off to the right and along the coast path. Unless your walkers already look tired, turn right.
4. Simply follow the coast path all the way to Porthcurnow. There are two steep descents and ascents on the path so you have to be reasonably fit, but the path itself is in good condition.
5. The second cove you drop down into is Penbarth. This is about halfway, if your walkers are too tired you can take the footpath up to the right, before you descend to the cove. This takes you past a campsite and back to the road. You can then get your walker's to put you on the lead and head right, up the road, back to the car.

6. Dogs are not allowed on the quay as this is still a working fishing port, so please take the alternative route kindly provided.
7. After the climb up from Penberth it is all flat walking until you drop down into Porthcurnow. If you want to take the bus home turn right up the valley and the bus stop is on the road running up the left of the huge car park. Otherwise, get refreshments and head back the way you came.

Bus Times:
At time of printing:
The 504 calls in Porthdurnow at 11.55 and 17.45 on its journey to Mousehole.
The number 1A (summer only) at 10:35, 14:35 and 17:40 and 23.00.
Call **0800 645 1420** for up to date info.

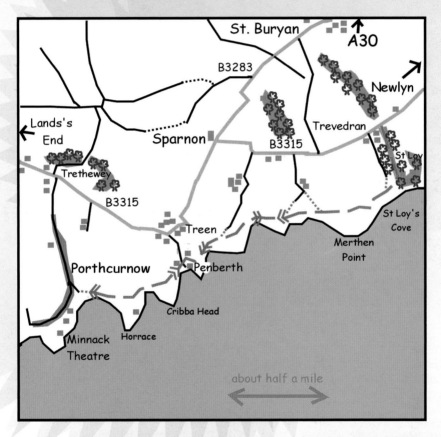

Playmates?	Y	Water to play in?	Y	Running space?	Y
Are there any hills?	YY	Any tricky stiles?	N	Car Parking?	N
Are farm animals likely?	Y	Poo Bins?	Y	Plenty of sticks?	N

Walk 11 - Tehidy Country Park

| Grid Reference: 642 437 | Landranger 203 | Distance: 2 miles (1 hour) |

This is a great place to walk the dog. There are loads of well kept, well marked paths that you can take around the woods, with lots of beautiful scenery.

1. You will find the North Cliff car park off the B3301 coast road between Hayle and Portreath, just north of Camborne and Redruth.
2. Once you find the car park, pull in and head into the woods. At the entrance there is a really useful map. There are a couple of different colour marker posts you can follow, from here we chose the path that led off to the left and followed the marker posts that took us around the edge of the woods.
3. After a long while you will bare round to the right and you will see a golf course next to the woods. As you follow the path along by the golf course you will eventually reach a four way sign post. We just kept following our coloured markers, but if you want to extend the walk and have some water fun you can head for the lakes via Otter Bridge or turn left and refresh yourselves at the Café (not always open). Once you have explored the other woods, come back to the 4-way sign and follow the markers back to the North Cliff car park.

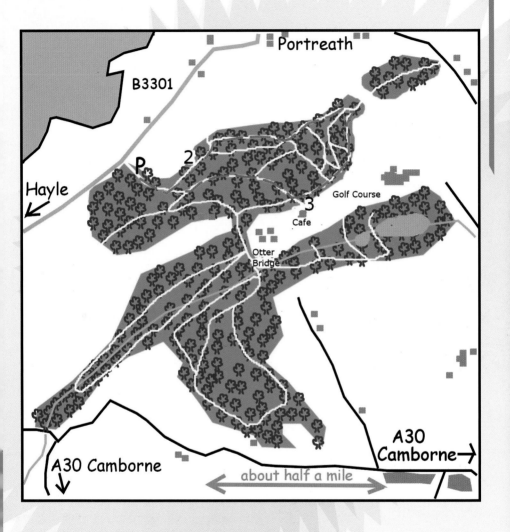

Playmates?	Y	Water to play in?	Y	Running space?	Y
Are there any hills?	N	Any tricky stiles?	N	Car Parking?	Y
Are farm animals likely?	N	Poo Bins?	Y	Plenty of sticks?	Y

Walk 12 - Marazion Marshes

Grid Reference: 514 312   Landranger 203   Distance: 1 mile (30mins)

This is a lovely little dog walk near Marazion with great scenery including St Michael's Mount in the background. It is short but we have included it because it is near lots of beaches with dog bans in the summer, so it is somewhere to let doggies stretch their legs

1. Follow the A394 into Marazion, as you approach Marazion you will cross a railway bridge, after this the road forks, take the left fork and park in the large car park on the right. You will see the marshes on your left.
2. Please make sure your walkers put you on the lead as this road gets busy.
3. Cross the road into the marshes. You must stick to the footpath as this is important bird nesting habitat and birds don't like us doggies sniffing around!
4. The path basically follows the stream up the right hand side of the marshland. Follow the path up along the stream.
5. After a short while the path will become wooded and there will be a turning off to the right. This heads to a dangerous foot crossing over the railway. We don't think this is a sensible route for doggies off the lead, and it doesn't lead anywhere particularly special, we headed straight on until the path stopped. Then we turned round and ambled back. There are some lovely benches along the way where my walkers had a picnic. There are also ice-cream vans back in the car park, yummy!

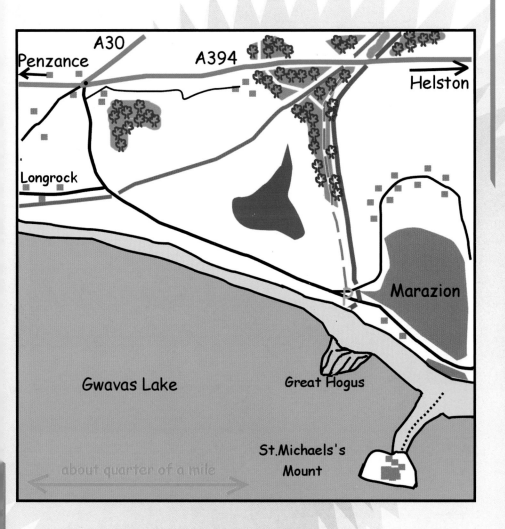

Playmates?	Y	Water to play in?	N	Running space?	Y
Are there any hills?	N	Any tricky stiles?	N	Car Parking?	Y
Are farm animals likely?	N	Poo Bins?	N	Plenty of sticks?	Y

Walk 13 - Cardinham Woods

Grid Reference: 100 667   Landranger 200   Distance: 5 miles (2.5 hrs)

This is a well kept Forestry Commission walking area with great facilities, well marked walks and lovely scenery. Worth going back to a few times! You can vary the walk you want to do depending on the time and energy your walkers have.

1. From the main A30 junction outside Bodmin you want to follow A38 signs for Liskeard, but make sure you keep your eyes peeled for signs on the left for Cardinham woods. They are not far from the A30 roundabout. Follow the signs.
2. Once in the car park you need to go to one of the information signs and decide which route you want to follow.
3. We started by following the Lidcutt Valley walk that gently follows the stream up the valley. We eventually got to a crossing point where there is both a bridge and a ford. I ran around in the ford whilst my walkers took the bridge.
4. We then followed the red marker posts up the valley that was straight in front of us once we had crossed the stream.
5. This is the Lady Vale Walk which climbs steadily up into the woods. There is a nice picnic area up here if you want to plan a lunch break. Continue to follow the red marker posts until the path winds back round to the left and down to the stream again. As you meet the path by the stream turn right and head back down to the car park on the opposite side of the river to the one you came up on.

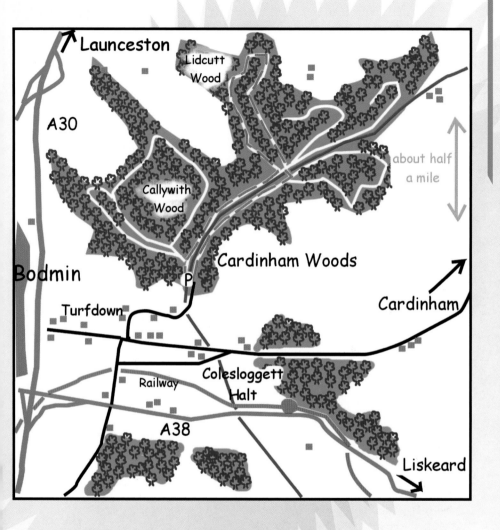

Playmates?	Y	Water to play in?	Y	Running space?	Y
Are there any hills?	Y	Any tricky stiles?	N	Car Parking?	Y
Are farm animals likely?	N	Poo Bins?	Y	Plenty of sticks?	Y

Walk 14 - Cotehele Clamber

| Grid Reference: 435 685 | Landranger 201 | Distance: 3 miles (1.5 hrs) |

This is a lovely riverside walk that starts in the lovely village of Calstock and ends at the quayside of Cotehele House on the banks of the Tamar.

1. From Plymouth head north towards either Callington (Cornish side), or Tavistock (Devonian side). Then follow signs for Gunnislake. In Gunnislake follow signs to Calstock. Drive right to the bottom of the hill in Calstock, turn right towards the river and park in the car park on the river's edge, next to the football pitch.
2. Now head out of the car park towards the Viaduct (you can't miss it!) Head back towards the hill you just came down.
3. When you reach the bottom of the hill start walking back up, after a few metres take the quiet road on your left that follows the river under the viaduct.
4. Follow this road along the river bank, my walkers normally allow me off the lead now, just keep an eye out for the odd car.
5. Eventually the road bends around to the right and forks. Ignore the footpath leading off uphill to the right carry straight on past the two cottages. You will then see an obvious path leading off to the left into the woods above the river, follow this.
6. Follow the path through the woods enjoying the great views of the Tamar. Follow signs that lead you to the Cotehele Quay and Mill.
7. My walkers tend to put me on the lead at the Quay otherwise I get a bit excited with all the people about. However, I sometimes get an ice-cream as a reward.
8. Once you have enjoyed the sights you can return the way you came.

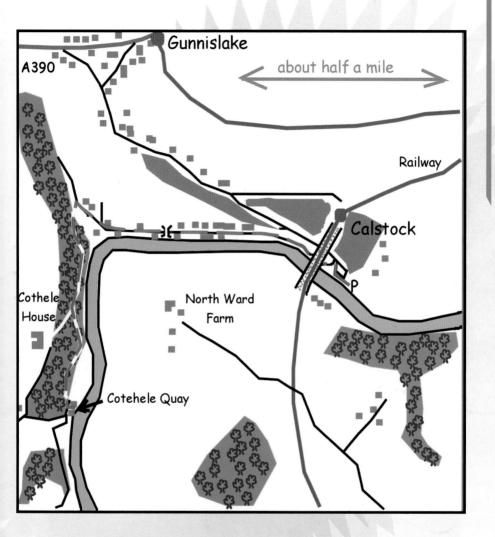

Playmates?	Y	Water to play in?	Y	Running space?	Y
Are there any hills?	Y	Any tricky stiles?	N	Car Parking?	Y
Are farm animals likely?	N	Poo Bins?	Y	Plenty of sticks?	Y

Toby's Directory

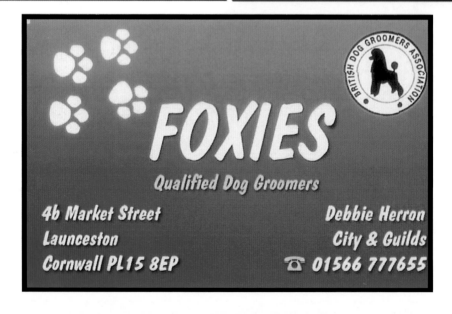

Toby's Directory

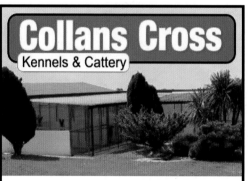